Journey Beyond the Veil

Journey Beyond the Veil

Vinu V Das

Tabor Press

© 2025 Tabor Press. All rights reserved. No part of this publication may be reproduced, distributed, or transmitted in any form or by any means without the prior written permission of the publisher, except in the case of brief quotations embodied in critical reviews and certain other noncommercial uses permitted by copyright law.

ISBN 978-0-9940194-2-4

whole persons in His presence.

Scripture provides vivid descriptions of the resurrection event. In 1 Thessalonians 4:16-17, Paul declares that "the dead in Christ will rise first," and believers who are still alive will be caught up together with them. This passage depicts a dramatic moment when graves give up their occupants, and the faithful are transformed in the twinkling of an eye (1 Corinthians 15:52). The physical remains, long reduced to dust or ashes, are miraculously reconstituted and raised to life by God's power.

This resurrected body is unlike the mortal frame that died. In 1 Corinthians 15:42-44, Paul contrasts the perishable nature of our current bodies with the imperishable glory of the resurrected ones. He writes that the body "is sown in dishonor" but "raised in glory." It is "sown in weakness" but "raised in power." Though it retains a true continuity with the earthly body, it is changed into a perfected, incorruptible form. This transformation frees the body from sickness, pain, and the effects of sin. It is immortal and suited for eternal fellowship with God.

During the resurrection, the soul, which has been enjoying the presence of the Lord, reunites with this newly glorified body. The intermediate state—where the soul experiences conscious existence apart from the physical body—comes to an end. The believer becomes a complete human being once again, composed of body, soul, and spirit in harmonious unity. This reunion fulfills God's design, as human beings were never meant to be disembodied. Rather, they were created to reflect God's image holistically.

The spirit, which has been in intimate communion with God, also rejoins the resurrected body. In the renewed state, the spirit's capacities for worship and fellowship are fully integrated with the resurrected body and soul. Worship transcends former limitations. The redeemed individual can engage every aspect of their being—mind, emotions, will, and physical presence—in praising the Lord. This restored unity echoes God's initial pronouncement that His creation was "very good" (Genesis 1:31).

The resurrection also signifies the believer's public vindication. Just as Christ's bodily resurrection demonstrated His triumph over sin, death, and the grave, so the believer's resurrection testifies to the same victory in union with Christ. Romans 8:11 states, "If the Spirit of Him who raised Jesus from the dead dwells in you, He who raised Christ Jesus will also give life to your mortal bodies." This underscores the direct link between Christ's resurrection and ours. When He appears, believers will be like Him, conformed to His glorified humanity (1 John 3:2).

The resurrected state brings joy beyond measure. No longer crippled by sickness or emotional anguish, believers experience wholeness in every aspect of their being. The longing for intimacy with God is satisfied as body, soul, and spirit collectively engage in perfect communion with Him. Relationships among the redeemed also reach an unparalleled depth, free from misunderstandings and conflicts brought on by sin. The entire resurrected community exults in love, unity, and worship.

1.5. The Body, Soul, and Spirit After the Judgment: Believer

Following the resurrection, Scripture points to a final judgment in which every person will stand before God. For believers, this judgment is not about condemnation but about the final confirmation of their salvation, accomplished by Christ's atoning work on the cross. The body, soul, and spirit, now reunited in a resurrected state, face this judgment in the fullness of redeemed humanity. The outcome is eternal life in God's glorious kingdom, where the faithful experience unbroken fellowship with the Lord.

Revelation 20:11-15 vividly portrays a scene where books are opened, revealing human deeds. Those whose names are in the Book of Life are spared the second death. For believers, Jesus' righteousness, not their own merit, secures their place in God's eternal kingdom. The judgment reveals God's perfect justice and mercy, magnifying Christ's sacrifice as the basis for salvation. In this moment, every believer's redemption is publicly affirmed, and their resurrection bodies, souls, and spirits remain forever in the presence of the Almighty.

After judgment, the believer enters the fullness of eternal life. Revelation 21:1-4 paints a picture of a new heaven and a new earth, where God dwells with His people. The curse of sin is lifted, and suffering, pain, and death are eradicated. In this eternal realm, the resurrected body never again faces decay or disease. The soul, which once wrestled with temptations and sorrows, now knows undiluted joy. The spirit, perfected through Christ's work, enjoys uninterrupted communion with God.

In this final state, believers experience the reality for which humanity was created. They worship God in an environment unmarred by sin. Their relationships reflect perfect love and understanding, free from jealousy, fear, or conflict. The unity of body, soul, and spirit enables them to serve, rejoice, and reign with Christ (Revelation 22:3-5). They live as fully restored individuals, contributing to the redeemed community's collective adoration of the Triune God. Each aspect of their being resonates with God's glory, leading to a harmony that surpasses anything known in mortal life.

The body's role in this eternal state is significant. Believers do not exist as disembodied spirits floating in an ethereal realm. Rather, they inhabit a tangible creation, described as a new heaven and earth. Their glorified bodies, imperishable and radiant, engage in activities that honor God. The physicality of the new creation affirms God's original design. Eden is, in a sense, restored and surpassingly enhanced. The environment reflects God's creative genius, while believers, in resurrected form, explore and delight in His handiwork without any hindrance of sin.

The soul, freed from the weight of guilt and grief, enters an everlasting rest. This rest is not inactivity but the fulfillment of all holy desires. The soul experiences complete satisfaction in God's presence, delighting in His character and purposes. Worship becomes the soul's highest joy, and learning about God's infinite nature stretches into eternal discovery. No longing remains unmet, for every God-given passion finds its ultimate fulfillment in communion with the Creator. This state of blessedness is unending, a continual unfolding of God's infinite goodness.

The spirit, perpetually united with God, exults in a depth of fellowship and love that words can scarcely convey. The Holy Spirit, who indwelt believers during their earthly lives, continues to dwell in perfect unity with their regenerated spirits. The awareness of God's holiness and love permeates their entire being. Joy, peace, and divine love define every moment. This everlasting union ensures that believers never taste separation from God, fulfilling Jesus' assurance that whoever believes in Him has eternal life (John 3:16).

In sum, after the final judgment, the believer's body, soul, and spirit dwell eternally in a new creation where God's presence is manifest. This glorious state brings wholeness and perfect communion, free from the ravages of sin and death. It is the culmination of salvation's journey, secured by Christ's blood and proclaimed in His resurrection. Believers, clothed in imperishable bodies, worship and serve God with undivided hearts and spirits. The result is everlasting joy in the One who makes all things new, completing the divine narrative of redemption for those who trust in Him.

If you found this message encouraging, please share it with others who may benefit. God Bless.

Chapter 2. The Paradise, The Heaven

Glories Unseen Beyond the Veil: A Christian Look at Our Heavenly Home

Heaven captivates hearts and sparks questions for believers and seekers. Scripture promises an eternal dwelling where pain and sorrow vanish. God's Word also presents vivid imagery of a realm where the redeemed live in perfect fellowship with Him. Many people wonder about the nature of Heaven, its location, and the qualifications needed to enter.

Heaven matters because it shapes Christian hope. Believers yearn for a home that offers rest from life's struggles. The Bible describes this glorious place in a language that both reveals and mystifies. It portrays a place filled with worship, holiness, and closeness to God. The biblical authors often shared glimpses of Heaven to encourage the faithful during trials, assuring them that the troubles of the present cannot compare to the glory awaiting them.

The doctrine of Heaven also affects how Christians live today. A correct view of eternal realities helps believers focus on the treasures above.

Jesus instructed His followers to store up treasures in Heaven rather than cling to earthly wealth. Saints throughout history endured hardship with the confident hope of Christ's everlasting kingdom. Heaven remained their goal, fueling perseverance and faithfulness.

2.1. The Paradise, The Heaven: Are they the same?

The word "Paradise" appears in multiple contexts throughout Scripture. Many readers encounter it for the first time in Jesus' promise to the penitent thief crucified alongside Him. In Luke 23:43, Jesus says, "Truly, I say to you, today you will be with Me in Paradise." From this passage, Christians infer that Paradise is a place of comfort and peace where the faithful enter after death. However, the question arises whether Paradise and Heaven are identical or different realms.

To address this question, we can look at the original languages. The Greek term translated as "Paradise" (paradeisos) derives from a Persian word denoting a royal garden or a park-like enclosure. When used in the Old Testament (in the Greek translation known as the Septuagint), the word often refers to the Garden of Eden, symbolizing a perfect environment where God and humanity walked in close fellowship. In the New Testament, the word "Paradise" appears in Luke 23:43, 2 Corinthians 12:4, and Revelation 2:7.

In 2 Corinthians 12:2–4, the Apostle Paul recounts his vision of being "caught up to the third heaven" and hearing "things that cannot be told." In the same passage, he mentions being caught up "into Paradise." This parallel indicates that Paul uses "third heaven" and "Paradise" as related concepts. Paul's vision suggests that Paradise and Heaven are interconnected, or at least that Paradise is located in the heavenly realms. Some interpreters see Paradise as either a section of Heaven or another term describing the same glorious domain of God's presence.

Revelation 2:7 references "the tree of life, which is in the paradise of God." This is reminiscent of the tree of life originally placed in Eden, the garden where God dwelled with Adam and Eve. The mention of "Paradise" in Revelation connects Eden's perfection with the renewed creation. This description implies that God's ultimate plan for redemption restores the intimacy and purity once enjoyed in Eden. Therefore, the "Paradise of God" describes the final state where believers reside in unbroken fellowship with the Lord.

Some theologians maintain that "Paradise" might refer to a temporary "intermediate state," while "Heaven," in its fullest sense, is the eternal dwelling place with God after the final resurrection. According to this perspective, believers who die before Christ's second coming experience conscious bliss in "Paradise," and then ultimately enter the New Heaven and New Earth after the resurrection. Others assert that "Paradise" and "Heaven" are essentially the same place, with no clear scriptural distinction beyond terminology.

In practical terms, Christians often use the words interchangeably. They view Paradise as a biblical expression of the state of perfect communion with God. The crux of the matter is that the faithful who depart this life immediately enter Christ's presence (2 Corinthians 5:8). Whether one calls this Paradise or Heaven, the most critical point is the promise of eternal joy with the Savior. Jesus' assurance to the thief on the cross reinforces that believers can trust they will be with the Lord upon death.

Any perceived differences between "Paradise" and "Heaven" should not overshadow the shared essence: they both point to God's dwelling, where His people experience rest, comfort, and immeasurable joy. The final fruition of this place of rest occurs after the resurrection when Christ establishes the New Heaven and New Earth. In that ultimate reality, God's people will reign with Him, free from sin and sorrow.

2.2. Heaven: Is it real?

Many wonder if Heaven is figurative or an actual location. Skeptics classify Heaven as mythological or a projection of human longing. The Christian teaching holds to the firm belief that Heaven is a genuine place. This conviction does not stem from wishful thinking but is grounded in Scripture. Jesus spoke of His Father's house in John 14:2, saying, "In My Father's house are many rooms. If it were not so, would I have told you that I go to prepare a place for you?" These words highlight the reality of Heaven and Jesus' active role in readying a dwelling for those who follow Him.

Heaven's reality emerges from Old Testament passages as well. The Tabernacle on Earth was a copy or a shadow of the heavenly sanctuary (Hebrews 8:5). Moses constructed the earthly tabernacle under detailed instructions from God, pointing to a greater reality in Heaven. Scripture thus indicates that a real environment exists beyond human sight. This pattern of earthly worship mirrors heavenly worship, reinforcing the idea that Heaven is not a mere idea but the original, perfect realm.

When Stephen was martyred, he saw "the heavens opened" and Jesus standing at the right hand of God (Acts 7:55–56). This event underscores the Christian conviction that Jesus, in bodily form, occupies a definite place at the Father's side. The open heavens that Stephen beheld convey more than a spiritual metaphor; they represent a tangible dimension where Jesus is alive and reigning.

The Book of Revelation also supports Heaven's existence as a real place. The Apostle John, while exiled on Patmos, witnessed a door opened in Heaven and beheld the throne of God (Revelation 4:1–2). John recorded concrete details such as a rainbow around the throne, living creatures worshiping, and elders casting crowns. These images may include symbolic components, but they also describe a realm brimming with activity, beings, and worship. The repeated references to God's throne room affirm that Heaven has structure, order, and recognizable features, though gloriously different from earthly realities.

Critics may argue that biblical language about Heaven is poetic or figurative. Certainly, Scripture employs images and metaphors to help finite minds grasp the infinite. Yet the consistent theme of a prepared place, a throne, angels, worship, and saints in God's presence suggests more than allegory. The Bible consistently presents Heaven as an actual domain where God's will is perfectly carried out.

Christians look to Christ's resurrection as evidence that bodily existence continues in a transcendent realm. Jesus did not vanish into a concept; He ascended bodily. He promised to return in like manner, implying that His current dwelling is not imaginary. Believers hold to the hope that they, too, will enjoy resurrected bodies in the New Heaven and New Earth (1 Corinthians 15). This renewed creation entails tangible features, including the holy city, the New Jerusalem, described in Revelation 21–22.

2.3. Things We Can See in Heaven

Heaven's wonders exceed earthly imagination, but Scripture provides glimpses of its contents. These revelations encourage believers to fix their gaze on what is unseen and eternal.

God's Throne and God's Glory: Central to Heaven is the throne of God (Revelation 4:2–3). John describes a throne encircled by a rainbow with the appearance of an emerald, symbolizing God's majesty and mercy. The One seated on the throne dazzles with indescribable splendor. Though no one has seen God the Father in His full essence, He has revealed enough glory for the heavenly inhabitants to worship continually, crying, "Holy, holy, holy" (Revelation 4:8).

Angelic Beings: Heaven teems with angels and other spiritual creatures. Cherubim guarded the Garden of Eden (Genesis 3:24). Isaiah 6 portrays seraphim above God's throne, crying out His holiness. The Book of Revelation speaks of living creatures around the throne with features resembling a lion, an ox, a man, and an eagle. They have wings and never cease praising God. Angels also serve as messengers and worshipers, carrying out God's will without hesitation (Psalm 103:20–21).

Elders and Saints: John's vision in Revelation includes twenty-four elders clothed in white garments and wearing golden crowns. Opinions vary on whether these represent the entirety of redeemed humanity or specific leaders. Regardless, they worship God, casting their crowns before His throne (Revelation 4:10–11). Scripture also presents a vast multitude of saints from every nation, tribe, and language standing before the Lamb (Revelation 7:9). These saints wear white robes, signifying purity granted through Christ's sacrifice.

Heavenly Sanctuary and Temple Elements: Hebrews 9 and Revelation 11:19 refer to the ark of God's covenant in the heavenly temple. This indicates that certain elements of earthly worship reflect heavenly realities. The mention of the golden altar of incense (Revelation 8:3–4) further suggests that worship in Heaven has structure and coherence. The heavenly temple is filled with the glory of God, and holy activities center upon His presence.

The River of the Water of Life and the Tree of Life: In the final chapters of Revelation (21–22), John witnesses a new heaven and a new earth. Within the holy city, the New Jerusalem, a crystal-clear river flows from the throne of God and of the Lamb, symbolizing life and blessing. On either side of the river stands the tree of life, bearing fruit in every season and providing healing for the nations (Revelation 22:2). This image echoes the Garden of Eden, suggesting a renewal of what was lost through sin.

The Lamb of God: Jesus, in His glorified state, is central to Heaven's worship. John sees Him as "a Lamb standing, as though it had been slain" (Revelation 5:6). The scars on the Lamb remind the redeemed of Christ's sacrificial death. Heaven's dwellers fall down before the Lamb, singing a new song of redemption. This continuous adoration of Christ underscores that Heaven revolves around the triune God's saving work.

Heavenly Light: God's presence illuminates Heaven. In the New Jerusalem, there is no need for the sun or moon because the glory of God lights the city, and the Lamb is its lamp (Revelation 21:23). Darkness cannot exist in the light of His holiness. The radiance of God permeates every corner, signifying purity, truth, and love.

These biblical descriptions, though partial, reveal that Heaven is filled with God's presence, holy beings, and redeemed saints. It is a realm of worship, purity, life, and immeasurable glory. Every vision underscores the centrality of God, as creation's greatest joy lies in beholding Him. The objects in Heaven, such as the throne, crowns, altars, and the tree of life, highlight that Heaven is not an empty void but a place where tangible realities blend with divine mystery. Believers await the day when faith becomes sight and they behold these wonders in unending worship.

2.4. The Three Types of Heaven

Scripture occasionally distinguishes different "heavens" rather than referring to only one singular dimension. The Bible's language about multiple heavens arises from the Hebrew and Greek usage that recognizes layers of the sky and beyond. While there is not an official dogmatic formula about these distinctions, Christians often refer to a threefold categorization of "heavens" based on biblical passages.

First Heaven: The Atmospheric Heaven

The first heaven refers to the sky or the firmament. Genesis 1:6–8 records the creation of an "expanse" that separates the waters above from the waters below. This expanse is what people see when they look upward: the air, the clouds, and the domain in which birds fly. Scripture often uses the word "heaven" to describe this visible atmosphere (Jeremiah 4:25, Matthew 6:26). This first heaven is the realm of weather, clouds, and the environment surrounding the Earth.

Second Heaven: The Celestial Heaven

The second heaven typically denotes outer space, the region of stars, planets, and other celestial bodies. Genesis 1:14–17 tells how God placed the sun, moon, and stars in the expanse of the heavens. In Psalm 19:1, David declares, "The heavens declare the glory of God," referring to the grandeur of the starry host. This second heaven stretches beyond our immediate sky and displays the magnitude of God's creation. It reminds humanity of God's immensity and power.

Third Heaven: The Dwelling Place of God

The "third heaven" appears explicitly in 2 Corinthians 12:2. Paul mentions being caught up to the third heaven, which he also calls "Paradise." This suggests that the third heaven is God's abode, the highest realm beyond the physical skies and cosmos. This is where God's throne resides, where angels worship, and where the redeemed gather in His presence. Jesus ascended to this realm, seated at the right hand of the Father (Hebrews 8:1).

Some biblical passages use the term "heaven" simply to refer to God's presence or authority, underscoring that He reigns from on high (Psalm 2:4). Distinguishing three types of heaven does not imply multiple final destinations for believers. Instead, it recognizes that "heaven" may reference different layers: the atmosphere, outer space, and the dwelling place of God. When the Bible speaks of the eternal home of the saints, it points to the third heaven, where God reveals His glory in fullness.

Bible teaches that, after Christ's return, the "New Heaven and New Earth" (Revelation 21:1) will unite the realm of God with the realm of humanity in perfection. In that consummated state, God's abode and humanity's abode merge, removing any separation.

2.5. Who Will Ebter The Pearly Gates of Heaven?

The phrase "pearly gates" arises from Revelation 21:21, which describes a high wall with twelve gates in the New Jerusalem, and each gate is made of a single pearl. On the gates were written the names of the twelve tribes of Israel. The question "Who will enter the pearly gates?" concerns eternal destiny. Scripture provides clear criteria for admission, emphasizing that Heaven is God's domain where sin has no place.

Salvation through Christ Alone: Jesus declares in John 14:6, "I am the way, and the truth, and the life. No one comes to the Father except through Me." This exclusive claim shows that Christ is the singular mediator between God and humanity. Entry into Heaven is not based on moral achievement, good deeds, or religious ritual. It is granted through a saving relationship with Jesus, who shed His blood as atonement for sin. Those who trust in Him for forgiveness and submit to His lordship receive the gift of eternal life (Romans 6:23).

Faith and Confession: Romans 10:9–10 teaches that if one confesses Jesus as Lord and believes in the heart that God raised Him from the dead, that person will be saved. This faith is not a mere intellectual assent but a deep reliance on Christ's work. Repentance from sin and turning to God in faith characterize those who are truly born again. The Holy Spirit indwells them, marking them for the day of redemption (Ephesians 1:13).

Holiness and New Birth: While salvation is through grace, the Bible repeatedly affirms that true believers undergo a transformation of character. "Without holiness, no one will see the Lord" (Hebrews 12:14). However, this holiness is the fruit of the new birth rather than a means of salvation. Good works and a changed life flow from genuine faith (Ephesians 2:8–10). Those who claim Christ but persist in unrepentant sin contradict the reality of saving faith.

Names Written in the Lamb's Book of Life: Revelation 21:27 states that "nothing unclean will ever enter [the New Jerusalem], nor anyone who does what is detestable or false, but only those who are written in the Lamb's Book of Life." The Lamb's Book of Life symbolizes the record of all whom Christ has redeemed. This divine registry underscores that salvation rests in the Lamb's sacrifice, not in human merit. Those who are Christ's sheep hear His voice and follow Him (John 10:27–28).

Obedience as Evidence of Faith: Jesus warns in Matthew 7:21 that "not everyone who says to Me, 'Lord, Lord,' will enter the kingdom of heaven, but the one who does the will of My Father who is in heaven." This does not suggest salvation by works, but it shows that genuine faith demonstrates itself in obedience. A merely verbal profession of faith without repentance or submission is insufficient. Authentic devotion bears the marks of righteousness, humility, and love.

God's Mercy and Grace: Even the most upright believers fall short without God's mercy. Every person, like the thief on the cross, needs the grace of Christ. The invitation extends to all who repent and believe. The father of the prodigal son in Luke 15:20–24 exemplifies God's open arms to returning sinners. Those who humbly acknowledge their need for redemption receive lavish mercy.

Thus, those who enter the pearly gates are sinners saved by grace through faith in Jesus Christ. They are washed by the blood of the Lamb, sealed by the Holy Spirit, and transformed into vessels of honor for God's glory. Their inclusion is not a reward for personal virtue but a gift purchased by Christ's sacrifice. The path to Heaven is narrow but freely available to all who call upon the name of the Lord.

2.6. Heaven and The Rewards of the Saints

Heaven is more than an escape from suffering; it is where the faithful receive God's promised rewards. Scripture uses the concept of rewards to encourage believers to persevere in righteousness. While salvation is God's gift, He also delights in granting crowns and honors to His children who have served Him wholeheartedly (Hebrews 11:6). These rewards reflect God's gracious generosity, not human merit.

Eternal Life as the Ultimate Reward: The primary reward is eternal life in communion with God. Jesus prayed in John 17:3, "This is eternal life, that they know You, the only true God, and Jesus Christ whom You have sent." Knowing God intimately and dwelling in His presence surpasses every other blessing. Heaven's essence is an unbroken relationship with the Creator. That relationship, restored by Christ's sacrifice, forms the core of eternal reward.

Crowns and Recognition: Several New Testament passages mention crowns for believers:

- The imperishable crown for disciplined service (1 Corinthians 9:25).

- The crown of rejoicing for those who share the gospel (1 Thessalonians 2:19).

- The crown of righteousness for those who love Christ's appearing (2 Timothy 4:8).

- The crown of life for those who persevere under trial (James 1:12, Revelation 2:10).

These crowns symbolize specific facets of faithful living. They reflect God's commendation for devotion, perseverance, and love. Believers ultimately present these crowns back to God in worship, acknowledging that all achievements flow from His grace.

Authority and Responsibility in God's Kingdom: Jesus taught in parables that faithful servants would be entrusted with greater responsibilities in His kingdom (Luke 19:17–19). These responsibilities indicate that Heaven may include meaningful service or leadership under God's perfect reign. Rather than idleness, Heaven features purposeful engagement in God's work. The joy of the saints includes participating in God's ongoing plans, exercising righteous authority, and glorifying Him through every task.

Inheritance of the Saints: Romans 8:17 calls believers "heirs of God and fellow heirs with Christ." This inheritance involves sharing in Christ's glory and receiving all that the Father has promised. Ephesians 1:3–14 describes how God has blessed believers with every spiritual blessing in the heavenly places. This inheritance encompasses the fullness of salvation, the redemption of the body, and complete deliverance from sin's effects. It culminates in perfect fellowship with God.

Different Degrees of Reward: Jesus states, "For the Son of Man is going to come with His angels in the glory of His Father, and then He will repay each person according to what he has done" (Matthew 16:27). Paul teaches that each believer's work will be tested (1 Corinthians 3:13–15). Those whose labor endures receive a reward; others suffer loss but are still saved. This concept of differentiated reward does not undermine salvation by grace. Rather, it underscores that God values the efforts and sacrifices of His people.

Eternal Joy and Fulfillment: Every reward in Heaven ultimately points back to the Giver. The saints will revel in the beauty of God's presence, worship, and service. Each believer will be wholly satisfied, free from envy or pride. Perfect love binds the redeemed together, eliminating any rivalry over differing rewards. All will rejoice in God's lavish grace and celebrate each other's victories.

Hence, Heaven represents both the believer's final home and the arena of divine reward. Salvation is the foundation, received by faith in Christ. On that foundation, believers build with acts of obedience, love, and endurance. God honors their faithfulness, reflecting His generous nature. Heaven's rewards motivate perseverance in a world filled with trials, reminding the saints that their labor in the Lord is never in vain (1 Corinthians 15:58). The Lamb who was slain is worthy to receive power, wealth, wisdom, might, honor, glory, and blessing (Revelation 5:12). In Heaven, the saints join that universal chorus, casting their crowns before His throne and finding eternal joy in the One who is worthy.

In Conclusion, Heaven stands at the heart of Christian hope. Its reality is anchored in God's Word, and its beauty flows from His character. Scripture outlines that Heaven, in the highest sense, is God's dwelling place beyond the visible skies. It is also depicted as Paradise, a realm of comfort and communion with the Lord.

Heaven is more than a destination; it is the consummation of God's redemptive plan. From Genesis to Revelation, Scripture testifies to a Creator who desires fellowship with His people. Through Christ, the gates of Paradise swing open once again. The Lamb leads His flock to living fountains of water, and God wipes away every tear from their eyes. This is the Christian's blessed hope. May our contemplation of Heaven awaken worship, strengthen resolve, and inspire earnest prayer that God's kingdom come and His will be done on Earth as it is in Heaven.

If you found this message encouraging, please share it with others who may benefit. God Bless.

Chapter 3. The New Heavens and The New Earth

"Finding Our True Home: Beyond the Veil"

The promise of the New Heavens and the New Earth stands as one of the most glorious teachings in the Bible. Many believers long for the day when God will transform creation and provide an eternal dwelling place free from sin and sorrow. The anticipation of a renewed cosmos is not a minor theme reserved for obscure passages. Instead, it appears in prophecies such as Isaiah 65, resonates in the epistles like 2 Peter 3, and reaches its climactic vision in Revelation 21 and 22. These scriptures paint a consistent and awe-inspiring picture: creation is groaning for redemption, and God has promised to restore all things in a way that surpasses our present comprehension.

This chapter seeks to outline the biblical foundation for the doctrine of the New Heavens and the New Earth, describe its characteristics, and clarify who will reside there. It will also address the significance of God's rules and governance in that perfect order. In addition, it will examine how believers can live today in light of these eternal realities. Scripture assures us that God's redemptive plan includes not only individual salvation but also cosmic renewal. While humanity longs for peace and justice, God has prepared something even greater: a future realm where righteousness dwells, love flourishes, and sorrow no longer exists.

Many people wonder how this eternal reality will look, feel, or function. They may ask questions about the continuity between the current creation and the new creation. They may wonder whether the resurrected saints will dwell in heaven, on earth, or in both. They may also yearn for tangible answers about relationships, culture, or daily life in God's coming Kingdom. Though Scripture does not present a detailed encyclopedia of every facet of the future, it gives us a trustworthy glimpse of what to expect. These glimpses serve to motivate our hope, our worship, and our commitment to holiness. They remind us that God's final plan is not destruction without purpose but transformation that fulfills His promises.

3.1. Biblical Foundation

The Bible begins with an account of creation (Genesis 1 and 2) and ends with a vision of a renewed creation (Revelation 21 and 22). This symmetrical structure underscores that God's plan was always to dwell with His people in a perfect environment. In Genesis, the Lord pronounces His creation "very good," establishing a harmonious world where humanity could enjoy fellowship with Him. Sin disrupted that fellowship, leading to spiritual separation, moral corruption, and physical decay. However, even in the midst of human failure, God promised a future redemption. This promise was foreshadowed throughout the Old Testament, culminating in the person and work of Jesus Christ.

The prophets consistently spoke of a future transformation that would affect all things. In Isaiah 65:17, God declares, "For behold, I create new heavens and a new earth, and the former things shall not be remembered or come into mind." Isaiah 66:22 reiterates this promise, linking God's name and His faithful commitment to a new cosmic order. These Old Testament oracles assured Israel that God's sovereignty extended far beyond the boundaries of a broken world. The future would not be dominated by evil, but by a divine renewal that would surpass past experiences.

The New Testament writers reaffirmed this hope by pointing to Christ's redemptive work. When Jesus took on human flesh, He inaugurated a kingdom that would eventually reach its fullness in the age to come. His resurrection served as the first fruits of a new creation. In 2 Peter 3:13, the apostle Peter writes, "But according to His promise we are waiting for new heavens and a new earth in which righteousness dwells." This statement connects directly to the Old Testament prophecies of Isaiah, showing the continuity between the Hebrew Scriptures and Christian hope.

The apostle Paul also highlights the cosmic scope of redemption. In Romans 8:19–22, he describes creation itself as "groaning" for the day when it will be set free from corruption. This depicts the entire cosmos longing for the culmination of God's plan, which includes the resurrection of the saints and the renewal of all things. Paul's vision reveals that salvation is not just about souls going to heaven. Rather, it involves an all-encompassing transformation. Heaven and earth will be brought into perfect alignment with God's holy character.

The last book of the Bible, Revelation, provides the most vivid depiction of the New Heavens and the New Earth. Revelation 21:1–5 describes a reality where "the sea was no more," symbolizing the removal of chaos and separation. John hears a loud voice declaring that God's dwelling place is now with humanity. He wipes away every tear, and death, mourning, crying, and pain are banished. Revelation 22 extends this vision by describing the water of life, the tree of life, and a city where God's presence illuminates everything. This completes God's ultimate desire to reconcile creation to Himself and to live among His redeemed people.

3.2. Characteristics of the New Creation

The New Creation described in Scripture surpasses human imagination, yet God provides significant details to guide our expectations. The most notable characteristic is the absence of sin and its devastating consequences. Revelation 21:4 declares that in this future realm, there will be no more death, mourning, crying, or pain. These words emphasize the removal of every effect of human rebellion. In the New Creation, the curse that once afflicted humanity is lifted. No longer will disease, fear, betrayal, or selfish ambition plague life. Instead, love, joy, peace, and righteousness will flourish.

Another defining trait is the direct, unmediated presence of God. Revelation 21:3 proclaims, "Behold, the dwelling place of God is with man. He will dwell with them, and they will be His people." This relationship will be free of separation or distance. Believers will enjoy a continual experience of God's presence, much like Adam and Eve walked with the Lord in the Garden before the Fall. However, this new fellowship with God will be even more profound because it will follow the full redemption accomplished by Christ. The veil that once concealed God's glory will be lifted, allowing a deeper communion than anything known in this present age.

In addition, the New Creation will display unimaginable beauty and harmony. Scripture uses symbolic imagery to convey its splendor. Revelation 21:18–21 describes walls of jasper, a city of pure gold, and foundations adorned with precious stones. Though these details employ figurative language, they reveal that the New Creation is not a shadowy or dull realm. Rather, it is a place where God's glory shines without hindrance. The environment will be radiant with color, light, and purity. It will be a realm of creativity, reflecting the majestic nature of the One who fashioned the universe.

The New Creation will also exhibit perfect order and peace. Prophetically,

Isaiah described a time when the wolf and the lamb would feed together, and violence would cease (Isaiah 65:25). While some debate the literal or symbolic meaning of these images, the core truth remains: every form of hostility, danger, and conflict will vanish. Relationships will be characterized by harmony and mutual love. Work will no longer be toilsome but fulfilling, reflecting our true purpose as stewards of creation. Music, art, and culture will express adoration for the Creator. Every dimension of life will overflow with worship, wonder, and gratitude toward God.

The transformation will be comprehensive, affecting not only the environment but also the resurrected saints who inhabit it. Believers will receive glorified bodies, free from decay or frailty. 1 Corinthians 15:42–44 explains that the resurrection body is imperishable and raised in power. These perfected bodies will be suited for eternal life, no longer limited by mortality or weakness. This transformation will enable believers to fully enjoy the blessings of the New Creation without hindrance or limitation.

Time itself will lose its current constraints. Though scripture does not say we will be timeless beings, it does suggest that the burdens of aging and death will no longer apply. Eternity will unfold in unbroken fellowship with God. While we cannot fully grasp how time will function in the age to come, we know it will be marked by continual joy and boundless opportunities to learn, serve, and explore the richness of God's inexhaustible glory.

The New Heavens and the New Earth will also be characterized by unity. All believers will share in the joy of fellowship with one another and with God. Denominational divisions or cultural barriers will cease to matter. The redeemed community will reflect every tribe, tongue, and nation, standing together in adoration before Christ (Revelation 7:9–10). This unity does not imply uniformity, because diversity will remain part of God's beautiful design. However, differences will no longer produce division or prejudice. Rather, they will enrich the corporate worship of the

Lamb.

3.3. Who Will Be Living on the New Heavens and the New Earth?

The Bible speaks of "new heavens" and a "new earth" (Isaiah 65:17; 2 Peter 3:13; Revelation 21:1), portraying a future reality in which God renews every aspect of creation. In this grand vision, heaven and earth come together in perfect harmony, unified under the reign of God. Although some theologians distinguish sharply between the New Heavens as the divine, celestial realm and the New Earth as the renewed terrestrial environment, others see them as overlapping spheres where God's throne descends and His people dwell in His immediate presence. Either way, Scripture teaches that both realms share a profound oneness, rooted in God's glory and shaped by His eternal purposes.

Revelation 21 and 22 describe a heavenly city, the New Jerusalem, descending from above. This city is adorned like a bride prepared for her husband. Its dimensions, as measured by the angel, are vast and equal in length, width, and height (Revelation 21:16), suggesting a perfect cube reminiscent of the Most Holy Place in the Old Testament temple. This imagery points to a realm of holiness, sanctified by God's immediate presence.

The occupants are, first and foremost, God Himself—Father, Son, and Holy Spirit—since the triune God reigns in majesty and glory. The angelic hosts also dwell in the heavenly realms, offering continuous worship before the throne (Revelation 4 and 5). The redeemed saints who have trusted in Christ will be part of this celestial community. Scripture speaks of believers being seated with Christ in the heavenly places (Ephesians 2:6), indicating a future reality that begins even now in a spiritual sense and will find its consummation in the age to come.

Some theologians distinguish between the New Heavens as the divine realm and the New Earth as the transformed terrestrial realm. Others see them as overlapping realities where heaven and earth merge in the final consummation. Revelation 21:2–3 suggests that the boundary between heaven and earth dissolves when the New Jerusalem comes down. God's throne and His people exist in perfect union. Hence, those who reside in the New Heavens are not separated from those living on the New Earth. Rather, there is a profound harmony between both realms, unified under God's sovereign rule.

In the New Creation, the moral law of God remains an expression of His character. However, sin will be absent, so divine commands will not function as prohibitions against evil desires. Instead, they will reflect the righteous and loving nature of God. In the New Heavens, obedience will flow effortlessly from redeemed hearts. The entire community of saints and angels will joyfully align with God's will. Rules, if we can even call them that, will serve as the perfect outworking of God's holiness and love, rather than constraints to suppress rebellion. There will be no rebellion to suppress because sin will have been eradicated.

The question of government in the heavenly realm also arises. Revelation 22:3–5 mentions that God's servants "will worship Him," and "they will reign forever and ever." This indicates a shared participation in God's rulership. Believers will exercise authority under God's supreme authority, likely in ways that reflect service, stewardship, and creative expression. There will be no oppressive structures or injustices. God's righteous governance will ensure that all responsibilities and privileges honor Him and bless His people. Those dwelling in the New Heavens will experience profound fulfillment and purpose.

3.4. Living in Light of the Future

The certainty of a New Heavens and a New Earth should profoundly shape how believers live today. Far from promoting an escapist mindset, the hope of cosmic renewal urges us to pursue holiness, serve others, and proclaim the gospel. Knowing that God will restore creation invites us to align our priorities with His eternal plan. We can invest in relationships, endeavors, and causes that echo God's redemptive purposes rather than chasing fleeting ambitions. This perspective challenges the idolatry of materialism, reminding us that we should not store up treasures on earth where they decay, but rather lay up treasures in heaven (Matthew 6:19–20).

Such future hope also influences our ethical conduct. 2 Peter 3:11–12 reminds believers that, in light of the coming judgment and renewal, they ought to live lives of holiness and godliness. This admonition implies that eschatology is not an abstract theological concept. It has ethical consequences, calling us to purity of heart, compassion for others, and devotion to God. Because we anticipate a world characterized by love and righteousness, we seek to embody those attributes in the present. We refrain from the world's pattern of selfishness and corruption, striving instead to reflect the holiness of God in every sphere of life.

Furthermore, the promise of the New Heavens and the New Earth motivates evangelism and discipleship. If God intends to bring a new order free from evil, then it becomes urgent to share the good news of salvation. People need to know that Christ's sacrifice paves the way for them to enter this renewed reality. Believers who grasp the magnitude of future glory desire to see friends, neighbors, and even strangers partake in that inheritance. This passion fuels missions and local outreach, compelling the church to shine as a beacon of hope in a dark and hurting world.

Living in light of the future also reframes our understanding of suffering. Trials, pains, and disappointments, though real and painful, become momentary afflictions when viewed against the backdrop of eternity. Paul emphasizes this truth in 2 Corinthians 4:17–18, explaining that our momentary troubles are preparing us for an eternal weight of glory. While this does not trivialize current hardships, it does offer perspective. The grief we endure now will one day be replaced by joy and restoration in God's consummated Kingdom. That assurance can sustain believers through persecutions, losses, and personal struggles.

A proper view of the coming New Creation also influences how we steward the environment and care for the world around us. Although the present creation is decaying, God's plan involves redeeming and renewing it. Therefore, Christians should not exploit or disregard nature. Instead, we should practice responsible stewardship, reflecting God's heart for His creation. This does not imply that we idolize the environment, but we do honor it as part of God's good handiwork. We remember that our labor in the Lord is not in vain (1 Corinthians 15:58). Whether through acts of mercy, service, or conservation, we can offer a foretaste of the future harmony that will be fully realized in the New Earth.

In conclusion, the promise of the New Heavens and the New Earth offers believers a profound and unwavering hope for the future. As we anticipate this glorious future, our lives today are transformed by the assurance of God's ultimate plan, inspiring us to pursue holiness, engage in meaningful service, and share the gospel with fervor. This future reality reshapes our values, priorities, and actions, aligning them with the eternal purposes of our Creator. Despite the challenges and sufferings we face in the present, the vision of the New Heavens and the New Earth sustains us with hope and resilience. Let us fix our eyes on this divine promise, allowing it to guide our worship, stewardship, and relationships. Ultimately, the assurance of an everlasting, perfected existence with God compels us to live faithfully, eagerly awaiting the day when His magnificent plan is fully realized. May this hope to deepen our faith, strengthen our love, and inspire us to honor God in every aspect of our lives as we look forward to the glorious inheritance that awaits us.

If you found this message encouraging, please share it with others who may benefit. God Bless.

Chapter 4. The Eternal Consequences of the Unredeemed

The Inescapable End for Those Who Reject Christ: Beyond the Veil

Death carries every person beyond the limits of earthly existence, yet the Bible assures us that physical death is not the end. Scripture reveals that even those who reject Christ will rise, body, soul, and spirit, to face judgment, emphasizing God's sovereign power over life and death.

4.1. The Body Right After Death: Unbeliever

At the moment of death, the physical body ceases to function. The heart no longer pumps blood, the lungs no longer draw breath, and the muscles relax. All biological processes halt. Scripture describes the body as formed from the dust of the ground (Genesis 2:7), underscoring its temporal and fragile nature. Once life departs, this earthly frame begins the gradual process of returning to dust, mirroring the finite design God has ordained for human flesh.

Medical science confirms that, after death, cells stop receiving oxygen, and organs break down. Blood pools in the lower regions of the body, rigor mortis sets in, and decomposition begins. These natural processes reflect the transitory state of the human body in a fallen world. The body's integrity declines without the animating principle of life given by God. While individuals may handle the body through burial or cremation, the scriptural truth remains that this vessel is no longer inhabited by the person's essence.

In Christian teaching, the body serves as a temporary tent that houses the soul and spirit (2 Corinthians 5:1). Believers and non-believers alike inhabit physical forms that are subject to mortality. However, the Christian view affirms that physical death is not the end of God's dealings with our bodies. Even for those who reject Christ, the body has a destiny in God's sovereign plan. Death ushers in the first phase of separation: the body is left behind in the physical realm, awaiting a future event when it will be raised for final judgment.

Nevertheless, there is no immediate glorification or transformation of the unbeliever's body at the point of death. Unlike believers who die in faith, non-believers do not experience a "blessed hope" for their mortal frame at this juncture (Titus 2:13). Instead, their bodies remain subject to decay. The dissolution of physical matter serves as a solemn reminder that life apart from God's redemptive grace ends in corruption. This reality echoes the consequences of sin introduced at the fall (Romans 5:12).

Funeral rites may vary across cultures, but each approach confirms an essential truth: the body has lost its life force. Whether placed in a grave or scattered as ashes, the mortal remains evidence of humankind's frailty. For the non-believer who has rejected Christ, this finality of the physical form signifies a stark separation from any comforting hope of immediate resurrection or eternal reward. Though the body's outward appearance can be preserved temporarily through embalming or other means, its ultimate fate is to disintegrate.

In many traditions, people honor the deceased body. Respectful treatment at funerals provides closure for loved ones. Yet, from a Christian perspective, the deeper meaning of the body's end is tied to the spiritual condition of the one who has passed. Bodies are part of God's creation, yet they carry the imprint of the curse that came through sin (Genesis 3:19). In that sense, physical death underscores humanity's universal need for redemption, a need that remains unmet for those who disregard Christ's gift of salvation.

The Word of God describes the inevitability of death: "For dust you are, and to dust you shall return" (Genesis 3:19). Non-believers who dismissed the gospel in life will see this truth realized in their physical frame. While the body alone does not define a person's full being, its decay testifies to the seriousness of rejecting God's remedy for sin. Those who refuse Christ remain in a state of spiritual alienation, even as their bodies lie silent on the earth.

In the immediate aftermath of death, the non-believer's body has no future hope beyond a future resurrection to judgment (John 5:28–29). It rests in the grave or is reduced to ashes, awaiting the appointed time when all the dead will stand before the Lord. The body experiences the natural cycle of decay until God summons it forth at the resurrection. That summons will not be to glory but to accountability. This truth should stir reverence for the Creator who holds power over life and death.

4.2. The Soul Right After Death: Unbeliever

According to Scripture, the soul constitutes the individual's consciousness, emotions, and personal identity. When death occurs, the soul departs from the earthly body, stepping into an existence that remains fully conscious beyond physical life (Luke 16:22–23). For non-believers who have rejected Christ, the immediate destination of the soul is a place of sorrow and separation, often referred to as Hades or Sheol. This realm is not the final lake of fire described in Revelation, but it is a holding place where the soul awaits the ultimate judgment to come.

Jesus alluded to this intermediate state in the parable of the rich man and Lazarus (Luke 16:19–31). While Lazarus found comfort in Abraham's bosom, the rich man who had lived for himself and ignored God's truth found himself in torment. Though this account does not establish every detail of the afterlife, it illustrates the reality of conscious existence for the soul after death. The rich man retained memory, recognized Abraham and Lazarus, and even displayed regret, suggesting that the soul does not lose its sense of identity or perception after death.

For the soul of a non-believer, the immediate experience is one of unrest. Having spurned the offer of salvation, it enters a domain of divine displeasure rather than divine favor. The Bible uses terms like "outer darkness" (Matthew 22:13) and "weeping and gnashing of teeth" to describe the anguish that awaits those who die outside of Christ. Although these expressions may be metaphorical, they highlight the profound distress that comes from separation from God. The soul, created to know and enjoy the Creator, endures the consequences of choosing distance from Him.

This state is not yet the final destination of the unsaved soul. Revelation 20:13 speaks of the sea giving up the dead, and Death and Hades delivering up the dead in them, suggesting that those who have died without Christ are kept in this waiting place until the final resurrection and judgment. This interim condition underscores the seriousness of rejecting the grace of God. The soul's capacity for consciousness implies ongoing awareness of one's lost state and the certainty of facing God's tribunal.

While in Hades, the soul has no means to reverse its condition. Scripture does not offer a second chance after death (Hebrews 9:27). The decisions made in earthly life solidify one's eternal destiny. The parable of the rich man highlights that there is a "great gulf fixed" (Luke 16:26) between those in comfort and those in torment. This chasm indicates the impossibility of crossing over or altering one's eternal standing once physical death has occurred. The soul of a non-believer, thus, resides in a place of sorrowful anticipation.

Some people question whether the soul sleeps or remains unconscious in this intermediate state. Yet biblical accounts, such as the parable of the rich man, suggest conscious awareness. There is no biblical text explicitly supporting a concept of "soul sleep" for the unbeliever. Instead, Scripture implies ongoing cognizance, which includes remorse, regret, and recognition of one's separation from God's presence. This reality underscores the gravity of Christ's warnings about eternal accountability.

Comfort and hope remain absent for the soul that rejected the gospel. The anguish comes from recognizing the lost opportunity for salvation and the impending confrontation with the righteous Judge. Such torment also springs from the realization that the greatest treasure—eternal fellowship with God—has been forfeited. Every earthly pleasure fades, leaving only the stark awareness of God's holiness and justice.

Though the soul's anguish is profound, it is vital to see that God's justice remains perfect. This intermediate state is not an act of cruelty but a necessary aspect of God's righteous government of the universe. Because He is holy, sin must be addressed. Those who die in unbelief have chosen a path that leads away from divine mercy. The soul's location in Hades is a temporary holding for the unbeliever, emphasizing the inevitability of final judgment.

4.3. The Spirit Right After Death: Unbeliever

The human spirit is often described as the breath of life, the immaterial aspect breathed into man by God (Genesis 2:7). At the point of death, the spirit leaves the body alongside the soul. Since the individual has died physically, the spirit no longer animates the body. Ecclesiastes 12:7 states that at death, "the spirit will return to God who gave it." This verse underscores God's ultimate sovereignty over every human spirit. Yet, this return does not imply salvation for one who refused the gospel. It simply acknowledges that God is the rightful owner and judge of all life.

For the non-believer, the spirit's departure from the body does not mean union with God. Instead, it highlights the accountability each person has before the Creator. Because the unbeliever's spirit was never born again, it remains in a state of separation from God. Some interpreters understand the "return to God" phrase as a figure of speech indicating God's authority over every aspect of life. Others see it as emphasizing that the life-giving spark is withdrawn. In either case, the non-believer's spirit does not find rest in the presence of the Lord but faces the reality of divine judgment.

When Scripture describes post-death consciousness, it typically references the soul's experience. The spirit, intricately linked with the soul, shares in the conscious awareness of the afterlife. The dimension of the spirit includes a God-oriented function, but for the unredeemed, that function lies dormant or corrupted. They have resisted the Holy Spirit's conviction and remain spiritually dead in trespasses and sins (Ephesians 2:1). That condition persists beyond the grave.

Some Christians hold the view that the spirit of the unsaved is simply confined to Hades alongside the soul. Others propose that the "return to God" is an expression of God reclaiming the life principle, leaving the soul in conscious torment. Either way, no biblical text suggests a second opportunity for spiritual rebirth after death. The moment of physical death seals the individual's spiritual state. If a person dies without being born again, their spirit remains unregenerate, confirming the person's separation from divine fellowship.

The concept of "spiritual death" underscores the tragedy of dying without Christ. While physical death is the separation of the spirit from the body, spiritual death is the separation of the spirit from God. For the unbeliever, this state of spiritual death continues beyond the grave. The spirit does not cease to exist, but it persists in a realm where God's presence is felt primarily in judgment, not in communion or blessing.

The Bible emphasizes the need for the human spirit to be made alive in Christ (John 3:5–7). For those who reject that offer, the result is a perpetuation of spiritual lifelessness. God's holiness cannot accommodate unredeemed spirits in heaven. Hence, the spirit of the non-believer aligns with the soul when facing a sorrowful interim. Both await the final resurrection and judgment, where ultimate destiny is pronounced.

An unregenerate spirit's immediate departure at death provides a sobering reminder that now is the only time to be reconciled to God. Hebrews 3:15 warns, "Today, if you hear his voice, do not harden your hearts." Post-mortem existence does not afford an opportunity for the unbelieving spirit to repent. The justice of God demands a resolution of every life based on decisions made while alive. For those who spurned Christ, that resolution is judgment, not grace.

4.4. The Body, Soul, and Spirit during the Resurrection: **Unbeliever**

Scripture testifies that all will be resurrected, both believers and non-believers (John 5:28–29). The resurrection is God's act of reuniting the physical body with the immaterial soul and spirit, signifying His authority over life and death. For believers, this event culminates in glorification. For those who rejected Christ, the resurrection leads to a different outcome: a reconstituted body prepared to face judgment. This universal resurrection underscores God's impartial justice and the truth that every person must answer to their Creator.

During the resurrection, God summons every person from the realm of death, whether the body was buried, cremated, lost at sea, or turned to dust. His omnipotence ensures that no fragment of creation escapes His power (Revelation 20:13). For the non-believer, the body that once decayed or disintegrated is reassembled. This resurrected form is not a glorified body suited for eternal communion with the Lord. Rather, it is a body fit for the solemn reality of judgment.

The soul and spirit, which have remained in a state of separation from God since death, reunite with this resurrected body. The conscious identity of the person is restored to bodily form, enabling a tangible experience of the judgment. This re-embodiment ensures that the entire person—body, soul, and spirit—faces the reckoning of sin. The resurrection is not a second chance for salvation but the stage upon which final accountability unfolds.

Scripture describes that the dead, small and great, stand before God's throne (Revelation 20:12). The books are opened, revealing each deed. The individual, now whole once again, must confront the record of unatoned sins. This moment magnifies the finality of rejecting Christ's sacrifice. Though physically alive again, the resurrected non-believer does not share in the joy of the redeemed. Instead, they face the fullness of divine justice.

Some have asked why God resurrects non-believers at all if they are destined for condemnation. The answer lies in God's commitment to righteous judgment and the inherent dignity of human beings as body-soul-spirit creations. Divine justice is not arbitrary. Each person experiences an equitable hearing. The reuniting of body, soul, and spirit ensures the entirety of a person is present to answer for deeds done while in the body (2 Corinthians 5:10). God's justice operates holistically, reflecting His perfect character.

The nature of this resurrected body for non-believers likely differs from the glorified body described for believers (1 Corinthians 15:42–44). Scripture indicates that believers receive an imperishable, incorruptible body suited for eternal communion with God. In contrast, non-believers' bodies, though resurrected, are not described as glorious or immortal in the redemptive sense. Instead, they are raised for the sole purpose of standing trial and experiencing the outcome of God's verdict.

During this resurrection, the soul that was in Hades or Sheol is released, but not to enter heavenly bliss. The spirit, which remained in spiritual death, is also brought into this reconstituted state. This reunion of body, soul, and spirit is an act of divine power that displays God's sovereign authority over life. Together, they stand before the Judge. No one escapes the knowledge and presence of the Almighty, even in death. In this moment, everything hidden becomes manifest. The reassembly highlights the undeniable truth that every aspect of a person's existence is accountable to God. Nothing remains concealed behind the veil of death.

4.5. The Body, Soul, and Spirit after the Judgment: Unbeliever

After the resurrection, every person stands before the judgment seat of God. For non-believers who have rejected Christ, this judgment culminates in a final separation from God, often referred to as the "second death" (Revelation 20:14). In that solemn moment, the full reality of divine justice becomes unmistakable. The resurrected body, conscious soul, and unregenerate spirit jointly face the sentence decreed by the perfect Judge who cannot overlook sin.

At this point, the opportunity for salvation has long passed. No further appeals, pleas, or changes of heart can alter the outcome. Those whose names are absent from the Book of Life are cast into the lake of fire (Revelation 20:15). This is not merely a physical torment but an eternal separation from the gracious presence of God. The body, once dormant in the grave, is now fully capable of experiencing the anguish of God's wrath. The soul, once in a temporary holding place, remains acutely aware of the judgment's finality. The spirit, never regenerated, perceives the ultimate loss: exclusion from the fellowship it was designed to have with the Creator.

The Scripture consistently portrays final judgment as real and unending for those who reject divine mercy (Mark 9:43–48). This unending separation testifies to the seriousness of sin and the holiness of God. The lake of fire represents the full weight of His righteous indignation against evil. The triune composition of the person—body, soul, and spirit—ensures that every dimension of existence partakes in the consequences of that rejection.

Unlike the intermediate state of Hades, the lake of fire is the permanent abode of those judged unworthy of God's kingdom. The agony is not only physical but spiritual and emotional. All residual illusions of self-sufficiency are stripped away. The body experiences suffering without relief, the soul endures remorse without consolation, and the spirit comprehends the eternal absence of communion with God. This threefold pain is the outcome of rejecting Christ's atoning sacrifice, which alone could have reunited the human spirit with God, cleansed the soul from guilt, and secured a glorified body fit for heaven.

Revelation 21:8 provides a sobering list of those whose portion is in the lake that burns with fire and brimstone. The emphasis is not on arbitrary condemnation but on a just response to hardened unbelief. God's love provided a way of escape through Christ. Those who spurned that love must face the alternative: eternal retribution. Jesus Himself warned of this fate, illustrating God's seriousness about sin and redemption (Matthew 25:46). Judgment is final because God's verdict is flawless.

In eternity, no barrier prevents the omniscient God from being aware of every person's condition, yet His favorable presence does not dwell with those in the lake of fire. Instead, they remain under His just wrath. The triunity of their being experiences the unending consequence of sin's wages. This outcome is not a testament to a lack of divine compassion. God extended compassion at the cross, inviting all to receive forgiveness. The final judgment stands as the inescapable result of a resolute refusal to embrace that gift.

Thus, after the judgment, the non-believer's resurrected body, conscious soul, and unregenerate spirit settle into an everlasting state of separation from the benevolent presence of God. The "second death" seals this fate. No further redemption is offered. The holiness of God remains untainted, His justice satisfied, and His love vindicated by the sacrificial offering of His Son. Those who rejected Christ experience eternal loss. In this stark conclusion, Scripture calls every soul to sober reflection and earnest repentance while the door of grace still stands open.

If you found this message encouraging, please share it with others who may benefit. God Bless.

Chapter 5. The Hell (Hades or Sheol): A Biblical Perspective

The Reality of Hell: Beyond the Veil

Hell, known in the Old Testament as Sheol and in the New Testament as Hades, is a subject of profound theological significance. It is frequently misunderstood, misrepresented, or dismissed as an allegory. However, Scripture consistently affirms the existence of an intermediate realm of the dead, where souls exist in conscious awareness until the final judgment. While many conflate Hell with the Lake of Fire (Gehenna), it is essential to distinguish between them. Hell, as referred to in the context of Hades or Sheol, is not the final destination of the wicked but rather a temporary holding place where souls await judgment. A proper understanding of Hell sheds light on God's justice, mercy, and the ultimate destiny of humanity. This chapter explores what Hell is, its biblical representation, its reality, what happens there, and who will go to Hell according to the Scriptures.

5.1. Hades or Sheol: the Same as Hell?

In the Old Testament, the term Sheol appears frequently to describe the abode of the dead. It is depicted as a shadowy, unseen realm where both the righteous and the wicked reside after death, albeit with distinct experiences. The righteous anticipate God's redemption, while the wicked endure distress. The Hebrew writers used Sheol to convey the concept of a place where souls remain before their final fate is determined.

The New Testament equivalent of Sheol is Hades, a Greek term carrying similar connotations. In Luke 16:19-31, Jesus presents a striking portrayal of Hades through the parable of the rich man and Lazarus. The rich man, upon death, finds himself in torment, whereas Lazarus enjoys comfort in Abraham's bosom.

Despite being a place of temporary confinement, Hades is not synonymous with Gehenna, the Lake of Fire. Gehenna represents the eternal state of punishment following the final judgment. The distinction is evident in Revelation 20:13-15, where Hades is described as being cast into the Lake of Fire after the Great White Throne Judgment. Thus, while Hades serves as the present realm of the dead awaiting final judgment, Gehenna signifies the everlasting state of condemnation.

5.2. Hell: Is It Real?

Many argue that Hell is metaphorical, serving as a figurative depiction of separation from God rather than an actual place of conscious torment. However, both the Old and New Testaments affirm Hell's reality. In Deuteronomy 32:22, Sheol is described as a place of consuming fire. Psalm 9:17 states that "The wicked shall be turned into hell, and all the nations that forget God." Isaiah 14:9 depicts Sheol as stirring with the arrival of the deceased. These passages confirm the existence of a realm where the unrighteous are held in anticipation of judgment.

In the New Testament, Jesus frequently references Hell as a place of anguish. He describes it as a realm of fire and torment (Luke 16:23-24), a place of outer darkness (Matthew 8:12), and a condition of separation from God's presence (2 Thessalonians 1:9). The consistent biblical testimony refutes the notion that Hell is merely a symbolic concept.

At the final judgment, Hell (Hades) will no longer serve its purpose as a temporary place of confinement. Revelation 20:14 explicitly states, "And death and Hades were thrown into the lake of fire. This is the second death, the lake of fire." This passage illustrates that Hades, having fulfilled its function as a holding place for souls, will be emptied and discarded. All who were confined in Hades will stand before God's throne, receive their final judgment, and be cast into the Lake of Fire, where they will face eternal punishment. Thus, Hell, as an intermediate state, will be abolished, while Gehenna will remain the ultimate and eternal domain of the condemned.

5.3. Things to Expect in Hell

The Bible provides vivid descriptions of the horrors of Hell (Hades/Sheol). Though full comprehension of its nature is beyond human understanding, Scripture reveals certain characteristics of this dreadful place.

Conscious Suffering

Luke 16:23-24 presents an explicit depiction of suffering in Hell. The rich man, tormented by flames, is fully aware of his agony. He experiences thirst, distress, and regret. Unlike physical death, where pain ceases, Hell is a realm where suffering is actively felt. The consciousness of those in Hell is undeniable; they perceive torment and experience emotions such as fear, remorse, and hopelessness.

Flames of Torment

Fire is a recurring image used to describe Hell's torment. In Luke 16:24, the rich man pleads for a drop of water to cool his tongue, indicating a state of intense burning. While the nature of this fire may differ from physical flames, it symbolizes overwhelming anguish. Jesus frequently spoke of Hell as a place where the fire is unquenchable (Mark 9:43), reinforcing the eternal nature of its suffering.

Separation from God

One of the most terrifying aspects of Hell is the absolute separation from God's presence. 2 Thessalonians 1:9 states, "These will pay the penalty of eternal destruction, away from the presence of the Lord and from the glory of His power." Unlike those who dwell in God's presence, the souls in Hell exist in a state of complete estrangement from divine comfort and hope.

Memories and Regret

The rich man in Luke 16:27-28 retains his memories. He remembers his earthly life and pleads for his brothers to be warned. This implies that those in Hell remain fully aware of their past and of the opportunities they had to repent but ignored. Regret compounds their torment, as they understand the consequences of rejecting God's salvation.

A Fixed Destiny

Luke 16:26 emphasizes that the gulf between Hell and Paradise is impassable. There is no possibility of crossing from one realm to the other. The finality of Hell is irreversible; once a soul is there, it remains in that state until the final judgment.

Weeping and Gnashing of Teeth

Repeatedly, Jesus describes Hell as a place where there is "weeping and gnashing of teeth" (Matthew 13:50, 25:30). This imagery conveys intense anguish, despair, and uncontrollable sorrow.

5.4. Who Will Go to Hell?

God created humanity to live in fellowship with Him, but sin separated us from His presence (Isaiah 59:2). The purpose of Hell is to serve as a temporary holding place for the unrighteous dead before they face final judgment. In this section, we will explore who will go to Hell and, more importantly, how we can avoid this fate by embracing God's gift of salvation.

The Wicked and Unrepentant

The Bible repeatedly emphasizes that those who persist in sin without repentance will go to Hell. The book of Psalms describes Sheol as a place for the wicked: "The wicked shall return to Sheol, all the nations that forget God" (Psalm 9:17).

The word "wicked" does not merely refer to those who commit outwardly evil acts like murder or theft. It includes anyone who chooses to live in rebellion against God. Wickedness, in biblical terms, is any action, thought, or lifestyle that is contrary to God's righteousness. Those who refuse to repent and turn to God will find themselves in Hades, facing torment and awaiting final judgment.

Those Who Reject the Gospel

Jesus Christ made it clear that faith in Him is the only way to avoid Hell. He declared: "I am the way, the truth, and the life. No one comes to the Father except through Me" (John 14:6).

Rejecting Christ is not simply an intellectual decision; it is a spiritual choice with eternal consequences. Those who deny Christ's offer of salvation remain in their sins, which leads to spiritual death and separation from God. In John 3:18, Jesus warns: "Whoever believes in Him is not condemned, but whoever does not believe is condemned already, because he has not believed in the name of the only Son of God."

It is not enough to be a "good person" by human standards. Many assume that kindness, charity, and morality will earn them a place in heaven.

However, the Bible teaches that salvation comes not through works but through faith in Jesus Christ (Ephesians 2:8-9). Those who reject Him, even if they lead seemingly good lives, will still face the reality of Hell.

Those Who Die in Their Sins

Hades is a place where those who die in their sins will await their final judgment. In John 8:24, Jesus gives a stark warning: "I told you that you would die in your sins; for unless you believe that I am He, you will die in your sins."

Dying in one's sins means passing from this life without having received forgiveness through Jesus Christ. After death, there are no second chances or opportunities to repent. Hebrews 9:27 states: "It is appointed for man to die once, and after that comes judgment."

This means that our decisions in this life determine our eternal destiny. There is no purgatory, reincarnation, or possibility of making amends after death. Those who die without Christ will be in Hades, awaiting their final judgment before being cast into the Lake of Fire (Revelation 20:14-15).

The Cowardly, Unbelieving, and Sinful

Revelation 21:8 provides a sobering list of those who will face eternal punishment: "But as for the cowardly, the faithless, the detestable, as for murderers, the sexually immoral, sorcerers, idolaters, and all liars, their portion will be in the lake that burns with fire and sulfur, which is the second death."

While this passage refers to the final judgment, it is important to recognize that these individuals will first be in Hades, awaiting that final sentence. This list includes not only those who commit severe crimes like murder and idolatry but also those who are "faithless"—those who refuse to trust in God. Even liars, a seemingly common sin, are included in this warning. The seriousness of sin should not be underestimated, as it separates us from God and leads to eternal punishment.

5.5. How Can We Avoid Hell?

God does not desire for anyone to go to Hell. In fact, He has provided a way of escape through Jesus Christ. The Bible affirms this in 2 Peter 3:9: "The Lord is not slow in keeping His promise, as some understand slowness. Instead, He is patient with you, not wanting anyone to perish, but everyone to come to repentance." Avoiding Hell requires taking intentional steps toward God. Here's how:

Recognize Our Sinful Condition

The first step in avoiding Hell is acknowledging our sinful state. The Bible declares: "For all have sinned and fall short of the glory of God" (Romans 3:23).

No one is righteous on their own. Sin affects every human being, and without God's grace, we are all destined for eternal separation from Him. Recognizing our need for salvation is the first step toward

Repent of Sin

Repentance means turning away from sin and toward God. It is more than just feeling sorry—it involves a change of heart and actions. Acts 3:19 states: "Repent, then, and turn to God, so that your sins may be wiped out, that times of refreshing may come from the Lord."

Repentance is necessary for salvation. We cannot continue living in sin while expecting God's grace to cover us. Instead, we must actively pursue righteousness and obedience to God.

Believe in Jesus Christ

Faith in Jesus Christ is the only way to escape Hell. John 3:16 offers the most well-known assurance of salvation: "For God so loved the world that

He gave His one and only Son, that whoever believes in Him shall not perish but have eternal life."

Jesus' death on the cross paid the penalty for our sins. When we put our faith in Him, we receive forgiveness and the gift of eternal life. It is through His sacrifice that we are rescued from Hell and brought into God's kingdom.

Confess Christ as Lord

Salvation requires publicly confessing our faith in Christ. Romans 10:9-10 states: "If you declare with your mouth, 'Jesus is Lord,' and believe in your heart that God raised Him from the dead, you will be saved. For it is with your heart that you believe and are justified, and it is with your mouth that you profess your faith and are saved."

Confessing Jesus as Lord means submitting to His authority and living according to His commands. It is not merely a verbal acknowledgment but a commitment to follow Him wholeheartedly.

Live in Obedience to God

True faith in Christ leads to a transformed life. Jesus said: "If you love Me, you will keep My commandments" (John 14:15).

Obedience to God's Word is evidence of genuine faith. While good works do not earn salvation, they demonstrate our relationship with Christ. A believer who truly follows Jesus will strive to live a life that pleases God.

Hell (Hades or Sheol) is not an arbitrary punishment but the consequence of sin and rejecting God's grace. The Bible makes it clear that those who remain in their sins and reject Jesus Christ will face eternal separation from God. However, God, in His mercy, has provided a way of escape through the sacrifice of His Son.

No one has to go to Hell. The choice is ours to make while we are still alive.

God's invitation to salvation is open to all who are willing to repent and trust in Jesus. Today is the day of salvation (2 Corinthians 6:2). Let us choose life in Christ and share the good news with others so that they too may escape the reality of Hell and find eternal life in God's presence.

If you found this message encouraging, please share it with others who may benefit. God Bless.

Chapter 6: The Lake of Fire (Gehenna)

A Place of Torment, A Call to Redemption: Beyond the Veil

The Lake of Fire, often referred to in Scripture as "Gehenna," is one of the most sobering realities presented in the Bible. While modern culture tends to downplay the concept of divine judgment, the Bible consistently affirms that a day of reckoning awaits those who reject God's grace. Unlike "Hades" or "Sheol," which denote temporary abodes of the dead, Gehenna represents the final destination for the wicked—a place of eternal separation from God.

Understanding the biblical teaching on the Lake of Fire is crucial for believers and non-believers alike. For Christians, it reinforces the necessity of evangelism, the gravity of sin, and the urgency of living a holy life. For those who do not yet know Christ, it serves as a warning of the consequences of rejecting salvation. This chapter will explore the reality of Gehenna, its timing, its nature, and what the Bible says about the experiences of those who will be cast into it. We will also examine Christ's warnings regarding this place of unquenchable fire and eternal torment.

6.1. Gehenna: Is It Real?

To understand the nature of Gehenna, we must first explore its origins. The term "Gehenna" is derived from the Hebrew phrase "Ge Hinnom" (Valley of Hinnom), a real location just outside Jerusalem, also known as Wadi el-Rababa. Historically, this valley held significant spiritual and historical meaning. It was infamous for the detestable practice of child sacrifices to the pagan god Molech (2 Kings 23:10, Jeremiah 7:31). This abomination led to the valley becoming a symbol of divine judgment.

By the time of Jesus, Gehenna had become a site where refuse, dead animals and even executed criminals were burned continually. The ever-burning fires and the presence of decaying bodies made it a powerful metaphor for eternal punishment. When Jesus spoke of Gehenna, His audience would have understood it as more than just a literal valley; it was a depiction of final, irreversible judgment for the unrighteous.

Some argue that Gehenna is merely symbolic, representing either a temporary punishment or an annihilation of the wicked. However, Scripture consistently describes it as an everlasting destination for those who reject God, and provides compelling evidence that Gehenna is not a myth but a real and dreadful place. In Matthew 10:28, Jesus warns, "And fear not them which kill the body, but are not able to kill the soul: but rather fear him which is able to destroy both soul and body in hell (Gehenna)." This statement suggests that Gehenna is more than just a state of mind; it is a place where both body and soul are destroyed.

In Matthew 25:41, Jesus speaks of the wicked being sent into "eternal fire prepared for the devil and his angels." Similarly, Revelation 20 describes the Lake of Fire as the "second death," where all who are not found in the Book of Life are cast into eternal punishment and that the torment in the Lake of Fire lasts "forever and ever." The biblical evidence overwhelmingly supports the reality of Gehenna as an eternal place of punishment rather than a metaphorical or mythological concept.

6.2. When Will the Wicked Burn in the Lake of Fire?

A common question regarding Gehenna is whether the wicked go there immediately after death or if they await final judgment. The Bible clarifies that no one is currently in the Lake of Fire; it is reserved for the final judgment.

When a person dies, their soul either enters God's presence (for believers) or goes to Hades (for unbelievers). Hades is not the final destination but a temporary holding place of torment, as seen in Jesus' parable of the rich man and Lazarus (Luke 16:19-31). The ultimate fate of the wicked is determined at the Great White Throne Judgment described in Revelation 20:11-15. At this event, all who have died without Christ are resurrected, judged according to their deeds, and cast into the Lake of Fire. This means that the punishment of Gehenna occurs at a future point in time rather than immediately upon death.

Furthermore, Revelation 20:14 describes the Lake of Fire as the "second death." The first death refers to physical death, which all humans experience. However, the second death is far more severe—it is eternal separation from God in the Lake of Fire.

The concept of the second death clarifies that the final punishment is not simply annihilation or a temporary purging of sins. Instead, it is an unending, conscious experience of divine judgment. This aligns with Jesus' teachings in Matthew 25:46, where He contrasts eternal punishment with eternal life: "Then they will go away to eternal punishment, but the righteous to eternal life."

The word "eternal" (*aiōnios* in Greek) is used to describe both life and punishment, indicating that both destinies last forever. There is no indication of an end to the suffering of those cast into Gehenna.

From the biblical evidence, the sequence of events leading to the Lake of Fire is as follows:

1. **Death and the Intermediate State** – The unrighteous who die go to Hades, where they experience conscious torment while awaiting judgment (Luke 16:23-24).

2. **The Final Resurrection** – At the end of the millennial reign of Christ, all the unrighteous dead will be resurrected to stand before God at the Great White Throne Judgment (Revelation 20:12-13).

3. **The Great White Throne Judgment** – The wicked will be judged based on their deeds and their rejection of Christ. Since their names are not found in the Book of Life, they will be sentenced to eternal punishment (Revelation 20:12-15).

4. **The Casting into the Lake of Fire** – After judgment, the wicked will be thrown into the Lake of Fire, where they will experience the "second death," a state of eternal torment (Revelation 20:14-15).

The fact that the Lake of Fire is a future reality rather than a present state emphasizes the justice and patience of God. He has appointed a time for final judgment, allowing opportunities for repentance until that day arrives (2 Peter 3:9). While the wicked face suffering in Hades now, their ultimate judgment is still ahead.

This also means that no human being has yet entered the Lake of Fire. Those who have died in rebellion against God are currently in Hades, awaiting their final resurrection and sentencing. Only after the Great White Throne Judgment will they be cast into Gehenna, where their torment will be eternal.

6.3. Experience in The Lake of Fire

Gehenna is described in the Bible as a place of unimaginable suffering, eternal separation from God, and irreversible torment. This terrifying reality is depicted with vivid imagery, including unquenchable fire, undying worms, darkness, weeping, and gnashing of teeth, symbolizing both physical and spiritual suffering. But what exactly can one see and experience in the Lake of Fire? Scripture provides many descriptions that offer insight into its horrors, emphasizing both the physical and spiritual anguish that awaits those who are cast into it.

The Sights of the Lake of Fire: A Place of Burning and Darkness

One of the most striking descriptions of the Lake of Fire is that it is a place of eternal burning. Revelation 20:10 states: "And the devil who deceived them was thrown into the lake of burning sulfur, where the beast and the false prophet had been thrown. They will be tormented day and night forever and ever."

This highlights two aspects of the Lake of Fire: its burning nature and its eternal duration. The fire is not a mere metaphor but a reality that causes intense suffering. The term "burning sulfur" (also known as brimstone) is used throughout the Bible to depict God's judgment, such as in the destruction of Sodom and Gomorrah (Genesis 19:24). This same kind of fiery judgment awaits those in Gehenna, except that it is never-ending.

Another terrifying sight in the Lake of Fire is outer darkness. Jesus describes it as a place where the wicked will be cast into "outer darkness" (Matthew 8:12, 22:13, 25:30). This suggests that while there is fire, there is also a profound darkness that intensifies the horror. Fire typically produces light, but the Lake of Fire is an unnatural, supernatural fire that burns yet does not provide illumination. This signifies complete separation from the presence of God, as 1 John 1:5 declares that "God is light, and in Him is no darkness at all."

The Torments of the Lake of Fire: Eternal Pain and No Escape

Beyond what one can see, the experiences in the Lake of Fire are far worse than anything imaginable. The suffering is both physical and spiritual, affecting the entire being of a person.

Unending Pain and Torment: Jesus repeatedly warned of the unquenchable fire of Gehenna, saying in Mark 9:43-48: "If your hand causes you to sin, cut it off. It is better for you to enter life maimed than with two hands to go into hell, where the fire never goes out. And if your foot causes you to sin, cut it off. It is better for you to enter life crippled than to have two feet and be thrown into hell. And if your eye causes you to sin, pluck it out. It is better for you to enter the kingdom of God with one eye than to have two eyes and be thrown into hell, where 'their worm does not die, and the fire is not quenched.'"

The phrase "where their worm does not die" suggests a continual state of decay, where the torment never ceases. The fire is never quenched, meaning that there is no relief from the burning agony. Unlike earthly pain, which can sometimes fade or be soothed, the pain in Gehenna is permanent and inescapable.

Weeping and Gnashing of Teeth: Jesus frequently described the experience of those in Gehenna as weeping and gnashing of teeth (Matthew 13:42, Matthew 22:13, Luke 13:28). Weeping indicates deep sorrow, despair, and regret while gnashing of teeth signifies rage, anguish, and suffering. This phrase portrays the emotional and psychological torment that will accompany the physical agony.

Imagine the overwhelming despair of realizing that one's punishment is eternal, with no chance of redemption. Those in the Lake of Fire will remember their opportunities to repent and turn to Christ but will know that they can never escape their fate. Their suffering will not only be external but will also include an intense internal agony of regret and hopelessness.

No Rest, No Peace, No Comfort: Revelation 14:11 paints a horrifying picture of the torment experienced in the Lake of Fire: "And the smoke of their torment rises forever and ever. There is no rest day or night for those who worship the beast and its image, or for anyone who receives the mark of its name."

The absence of rest means that suffering continues endlessly without relief. On earth, even the worst pain or sorrow can be relieved by sleep, time, or medical treatment, but in the Lake of Fire, there is no relief, no medicine, no sleep, and no escape.

Isaiah 57:20-21 also highlights the eternal unrest of the wicked: "But the wicked are like the tossing sea, which cannot rest, whose waves cast up mire and mud. 'There is no peace,' says my God, 'for the wicked.'"

In Gehenna, there is no peace, no comfort, no moment of reprieve—only constant torment.

Is There Any Escape from the Lake of Fire?

One of the most horrifying aspects of the Lake of Fire is its eternal nature. Unlike other forms of suffering that eventually come to an end, the punishment in Gehenna is everlasting. Revelation 20:15 makes it clear that those whose names are not found in the Book of Life will be cast into the Lake of Fire, with no second chance for redemption.

Many people hope that those in Gehenna will eventually be annihilated or given another chance, but Scripture provides no such indication. Jesus' warning in Matthew 25:46 states: "Then they will go away to eternal punishment, but the righteous to eternal life."

The word "eternal" (*aiōnios* in Greek) is used for both punishment and life, meaning that just as eternal life is never-ending, so is eternal punishment. There is no escape, no second chance, and no possibility of release once someone is cast into Gehenna.

In conclusion, The Lake of Fire, or Gehenna, is the ultimate and eternal judgment for those who reject God's salvation. It is not a temporary place of correction but a final and irreversible destination where the wicked will experience unending suffering, torment, and separation from God. Scripture vividly describes it as a place of unquenchable fire, darkness, weeping, and gnashing of teeth, emphasizing the terrifying reality of eternal punishment. However, this judgment is not God's desire for humanity, as He does not take pleasure in the death of the wicked (Ezekiel 33:11). The Lake of Fire was originally prepared for the devil and his angels, not for mankind (Matthew 25:41). Yet, those who reject Christ will share in the punishment of Satan, the beast, and the false prophet, who will be tormented day and night forever. This truth underscores the seriousness of rejecting God's offer of salvation through Jesus Christ.

Despite the dreadful reality of the Lake of Fire, there is hope—a hope found only in Jesus Christ, the Savior of the world. Through His death on the cross and His resurrection, Jesus has made a way for all people to escape this eternal punishment and receive the gift of eternal life. He bore the wrath of God upon Himself so that no one would have to endure it in Gehenna. As John 3:16 declares, "For God so loved the world that He gave His only begotten Son, that whosoever believes in Him should not perish but have everlasting life."

Those who place their faith in Jesus are rescued from the coming judgment and are given the assurance of eternal life with God. He is the Good Shepherd who lays down His life for His sheep, desiring that none should perish but that all should come to repentance (2 Peter 3:9). His arms remain open to all who will turn from their sin and trust in Him for salvation. No one has to enter the Lake of Fire, for God has provided the way of escape through the cross of Christ.

The invitation to eternal life is available to all people, regardless of their past sins or failures. Through Jesus, there is forgiveness, restoration, and redemption. The gospel is the power of God for salvation to everyone who believes (Romans 1:16). Those who accept Christ's sacrifice will never taste the horrors of the second death but will instead enter into the joy of their Lord.

This message should stir every believer to urgency in evangelism, knowing that countless souls are heading toward eternal destruction. The Great Commission is a call to rescue the perishing, to proclaim the good news of salvation, and to turn people from darkness to light. Jesus is the only hope for mankind, and His gospel must be preached boldly and faithfully.

For those who are still uncertain, the time to turn to Jesus is now, for tomorrow is not promised. The Bible warns that today is the day of salvation (2 Corinthians 6:2). No one knows when their last breath will be, and once a person enters eternity, there is no second chance. Choosing Christ means choosing eternal joy, peace, and fellowship with God, while rejecting Him leads to eternal separation in the Lake of Fire.

Let this truth lead every believer to worship, gratitude, and a deep love for the Savior who delivered us from such a terrifying fate. Jesus' sacrifice is our greatest hope, and through Him, we have the assurance of everlasting life. One day, those who trust in Him will dwell in the New Heaven and New Earth, where there is no more pain, sorrow, or death (Revelation 21:4).

May this message be a call to repentance, a warning to the lost, and a comfort to the redeemed. For those who are in Christ, there is no fear of the Lake of Fire, only the joyful expectation of eternity with God. This is the promise of our faithful Lord, and it is a promise that will never fail. Come to Jesus today, for He alone is the way, the truth, and the life.

If you found this message encouraging, please share it with others who may benefit. God Bless.

www.ingramcontent.com/pod-product-compliance
Lightning Source LLC
Chambersburg PA
CBHW070800050426
42452CB00012B/2426